ANIMALS IN DANGER!

Bengal Tigers

Nancy Dickmann

BROWN BEAR BOOKS

Published by Brown Bear Books Ltd
4877 N. Circulo Bujia
Tucson, AZ 85718
USA

and

Unit 1/D, Leroy House
436 Essex Rd
London N1 3QP
UK

ISBN 978-1-78121-440-4 (library bound)
ISBN 978-1-78121-462-6 (paperback)

Library of Congress Cataloging-in-Publication Data available on request

Text: Nancy Dickmann
Designer: Supriya Sahai
Design Manager: Keith Davis
Picture Researcher: Laila Torsun
Editorial Director: Lindsey Lowe
Children's Publisher: Anne O'Daly

Manufactured in the United States of America
CPSIA compliance information: Batch#AG/5623

Picture Credits
The photographs in this book are used by permission and through the courtesy of:

Front Cover: iStock: The Palmer.
123rf: Valdimir Cech 20; Alamy: Mark Daffey 16–17; Dreamstime: Abhishek Singh 1, Julian W 8–9; Getty Images: Renee Lynn/Corbis/VCG 12–13; iStock: greenapeture 14–15, natbits 18–19, Photocech 8, 10–11, Prasanna S 18; Shutterstock: 14, Patrick Foto 6–7, Guan Jiangchi 10, Cynthia Kidwell 12, nellsky 5, Offical 4, Raju Soni 21, Tradol 16.

All other artwork and photography © Brown Bear Books.

t-top, r-right, l-left, c-center, b-bottom

Brown Bear Books has made every attempt to contact the copyright holder. If you have any information please contact: licensing@brownbearbooks.co.uk

Websites
The website addresses in this book were valid at the time of going to press. However, it is possible that contents or addresses may change following publication of this book. No responsibility for any such changes can be accepted by the author or the publisher. Readers should be supervised when they access the Internet.

Words in **bold** appear in the Useful Words on page 23.

Contents

What Are Bengal Tigers?

Bengal tigers are a type of cat. They are related to lions and leopards. They are also related to pet cats. But tigers are much bigger and stronger. They are the largest cats in the world.

Pet cats are in the same family as tigers.

IN DANGER!

Bengal tigers are in danger of dying out. People need to protect them.

Tigers are **mammals**. Their bodies are covered in fur. They make milk for their young. Like all cats, they have claws and whiskers.

Tiger Habitats

A **habitat** is the place where an animal lives. Most Bengal tigers live in India and nearby countries. They live in **grasslands** and forests. Some of the forests are dry. Others are hot, wet rain forests.

Bengal tigers only live in the southern part of Asia.

Bengal tigers also live in **mangrove swamps**. These watery habitats are on the coast. The roots of trees reach into the water. Fish and other animals hide in the long roots.

WOW!

Bengal tigers are good swimmers. The water helps them stay cool.

Finding Food

Tigers are **carnivores**. They eat meat. Bengal tigers hunt deer and antelope. They also eat monkeys and wild pigs. Tigers sometimes kill farm animals, or even humans.

Bengal tigers even eat porcupines.

Tigers sometimes steal food from other cats. They might hide leftovers to eat later. After a big meal, a tiger might not eat again for several days.

Super Stripes

A tiger's belly is white. The rest of its body is orange. It has black stripes. Tigers are the only big cats that have stripes.

A few Bengal tigers are white and black. They still have stripes.

WOW!

No two tigers have the exact same pattern of stripes.

Tigers sneak up on their **prey**. They move closer, slowly and silently. Then they pounce! Stripes help a tiger hide in long grass. Prey animals can't easily spot it.

Baby Tigers

Baby tigers are called cubs. A mother tiger usually has two to four cubs. The cubs are small and stripy. At first, they are blind. The mother tiger keeps them safe.

Tiger cubs play while their mother hunts.
After a few months, the cubs are bigger.
They can go hunting with their mom.
She shows them how to catch food.

Tigers in Danger

Bengal tigers are at risk of dying out. They are **endangered**. For many years, people hunted them. They wanted to kill a dangerous animal.

People turn tiger skins into rugs.

Tigers were nearly wiped out. There are very few left. The forests where they live are shrinking. People cut down the forests. They sell the wood. They use the land for farming.

Helping Tigers

There are laws to protect tigers.
But **poachers** still kill them.
They sell their body parts.
Farmers sometimes kill tigers
to protect their animals.

In some places, people sell lucky charms made from tiger bones or teeth.

In national parks, **rangers** protect tigers. They try to stop poachers. Scientists count tigers. They check they are healthy. Other people work to protect the forest **habitat**.

WOW!

Some park rangers ride elephants to watch for poachers.

What's Next?

There are about 2,500 wild Bengal tigers left. Their numbers are going down. Poaching is a big problem. Selling tiger parts is **illegal**. But people pay high prices for them.

Many tigers live in protected areas.

Tigers need a lot of land. They need enough animals to hunt. When forests are lost, there is less **prey**. People need to protect tigers. They need to protect their **habitats**, too.

Bengal Tiger Helpers

These groups help Bengal tigers:

The International Union for Conservation of Nature (IUCN) is a group of scientists. The scientists count animals. They keep track of their numbers. They decide whether an animal is **endangered**. They say when it has gone **extinct**.

The WWF is a charity. It helps protect forests where tigers live.

Tigers Forever is a charity. It helps train park **rangers**.

Fact File

Average life span in the wild: 10 years

Size: 7–9 feet
(2.1–2.7 meters) long,
including the tail

Weight: 240–500 pounds
(109–227 kilograms)

Diet: meat

Teeth: up to 3 inches
(8 centimeters) long

WOW!

A tiger's roar can be heard 1.8 miles (3 km) away.

Try It!

Imagine that you are a scientist. You have set up a hidden camera in the forest. Which animals has it snapped? Make a bar graph to show its results.

You will need:

- graph paper
- pencil
- ruler
- colored pencils

Animal	number seen
Bengal Tiger	2
Water Buffalo	1
Monkey	8
Deer	5
Wild Pig	3

1 Write "Animal" at the bottom of the graph. Write the animals on the line. They should be evenly spaced.

2 Along the side, write "Number seen." Write in numbers from 1 to 10.

3 Look at the data in the table. For each animal, plot the number on the graph.

4 Use the ruler to make a bar for each animal. Color it in. Which animal has the highest bar?

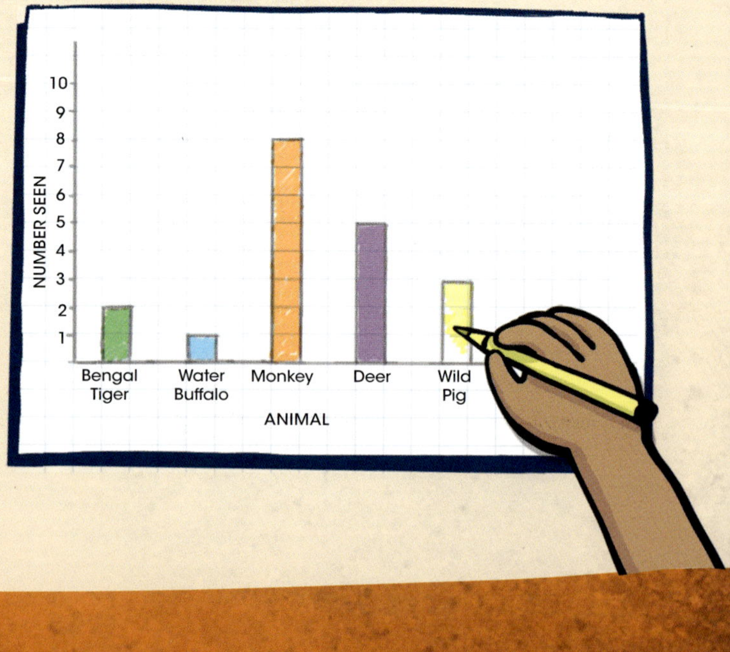

Useful Words

carnivore An animal that eats meat.

endangered In danger of dying out completely so that no more are left.

extinct Having died out completely so that no more are left.

grassland An area of land covered in grasses, with few trees.

habitat The place where a plant or animal lives.

illegal Against the law.

mammal Member of a group of animals that have fur and make milk for their young.

mangrove swamp An area on the coast where mangrove trees and other plants grow.

poacher A person who hunts or traps animals when it is against the law.

prey An animal that is hunted and eaten by other types of animals.

ranger A person whose job is patrolling a park or forest to keep animals safe.

Find Out More

Websites

www.bbc.co.uk/news/science-environment-31869772

www.nationalgeographic.com/animals/mammals/b/bengal-tiger/

www.worldwildlife.org/species/bengal-tiger

Books

Bengal Tigers Are Awesome! Megan C. Peterson, Capstone Press, 2015

Lion vs. Tiger Isabel Thomas, Heinemann, 2017

Tigers Jill Esbaum, National Geographic Children's Books, 2016

Index